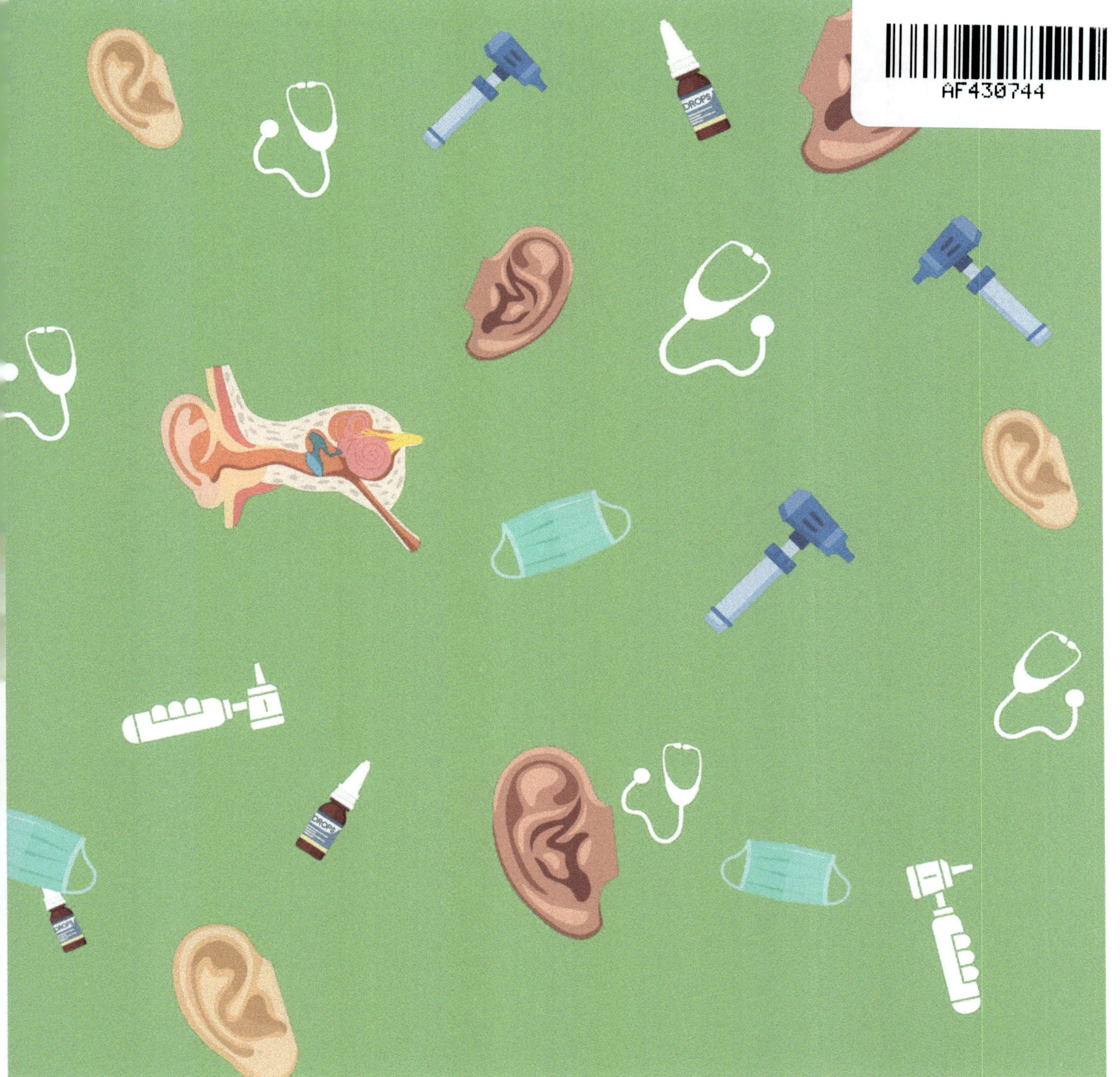

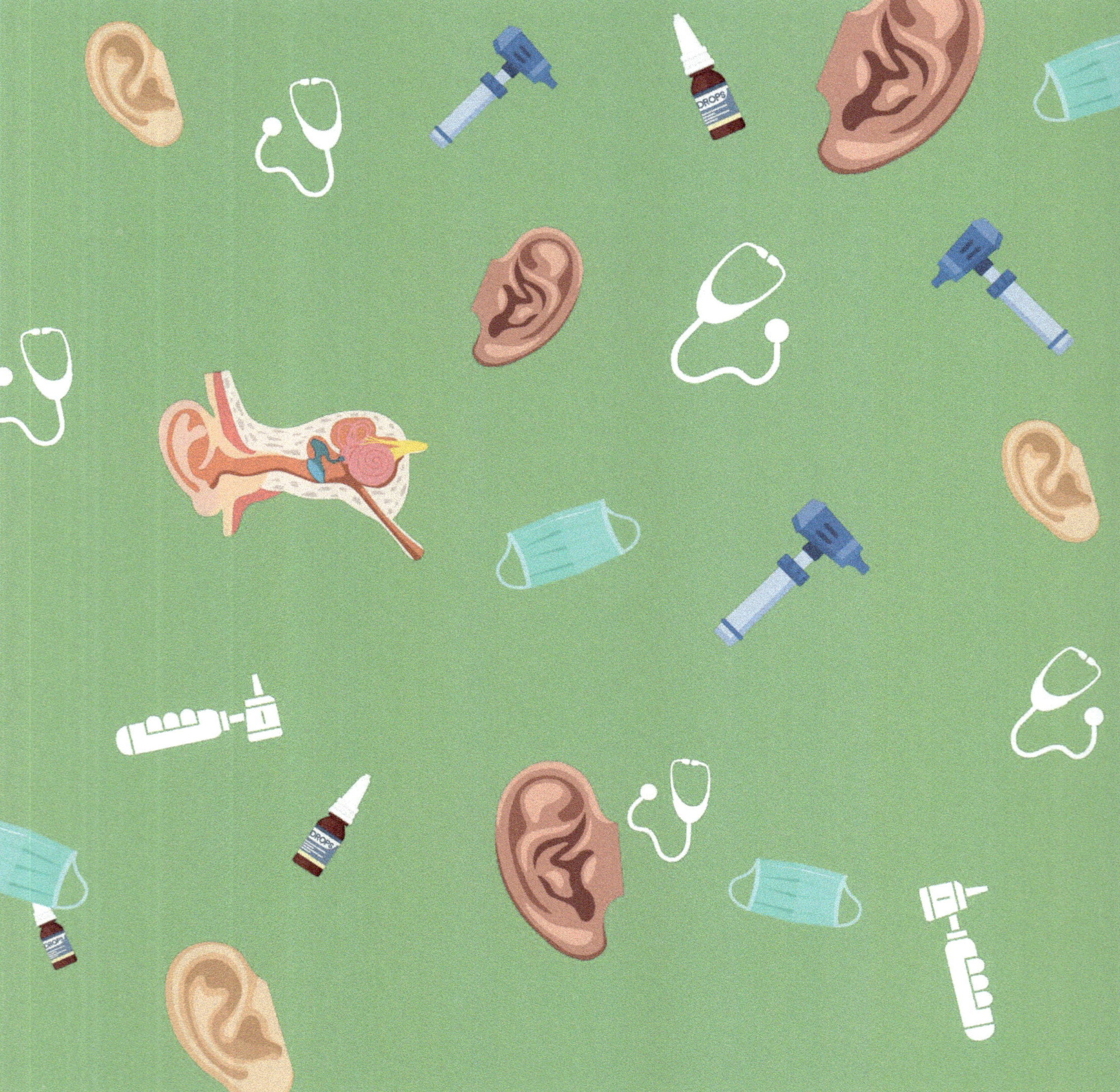

EARS, TUBES and the EAR-RIFFIC DOCTOR

By: ABDashnaw

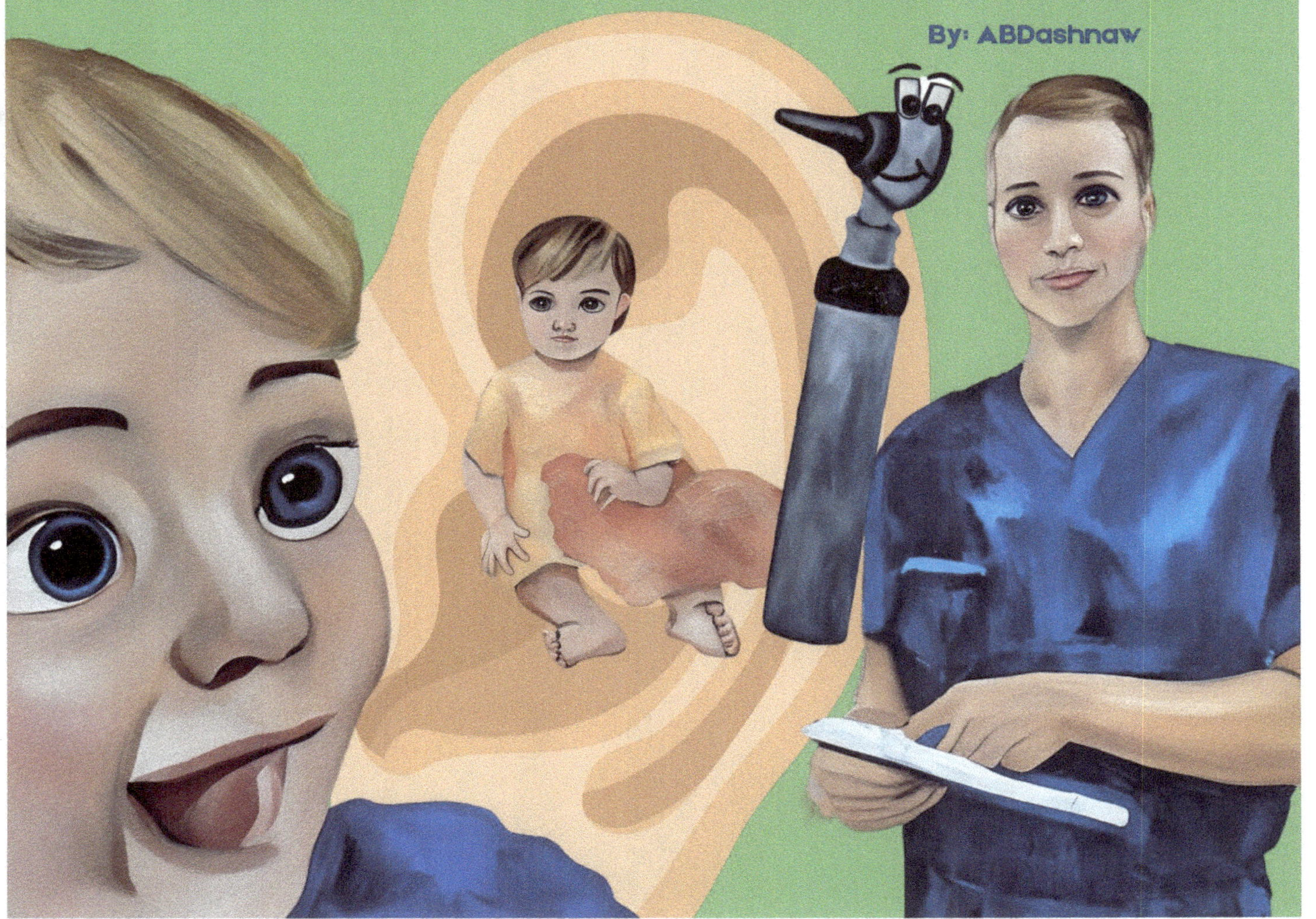

Written and Illustrated by ABDashnaw
Collaborated with Dr. Justin Way, M.D. and Dr. Zachary Griggs, DO

Ears, Tubes and The Ear-riffic Doctor is a children's book for
enjoyment, preparation and learning. Please consult your pediatrician
for recommended treatment.

Copyright 2024

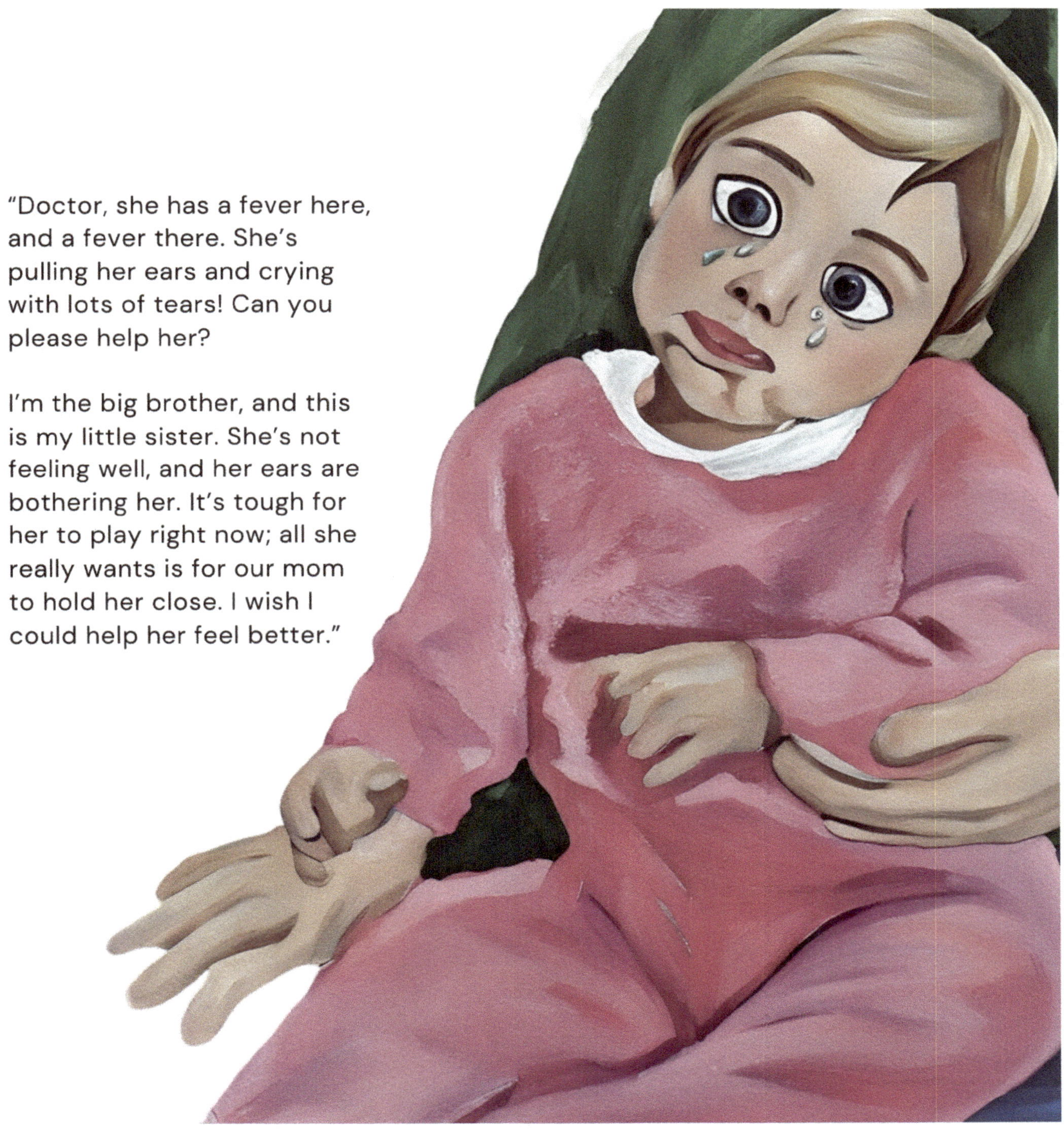

"Doctor, she has a fever here, and a fever there. She's pulling her ears and crying with lots of tears! Can you please help her?

I'm the big brother, and this is my little sister. She's not feeling well, and her ears are bothering her. It's tough for her to play right now; all she really wants is for our mom to hold her close. I wish I could help her feel better."

"Let's take a look," said the Doctor. On the counter were a few objects for the doctor to use. I looked over at them. They were shiny, cone shaped and different sizes. "Doctor, what are those?" I asked, pointing at the counter.

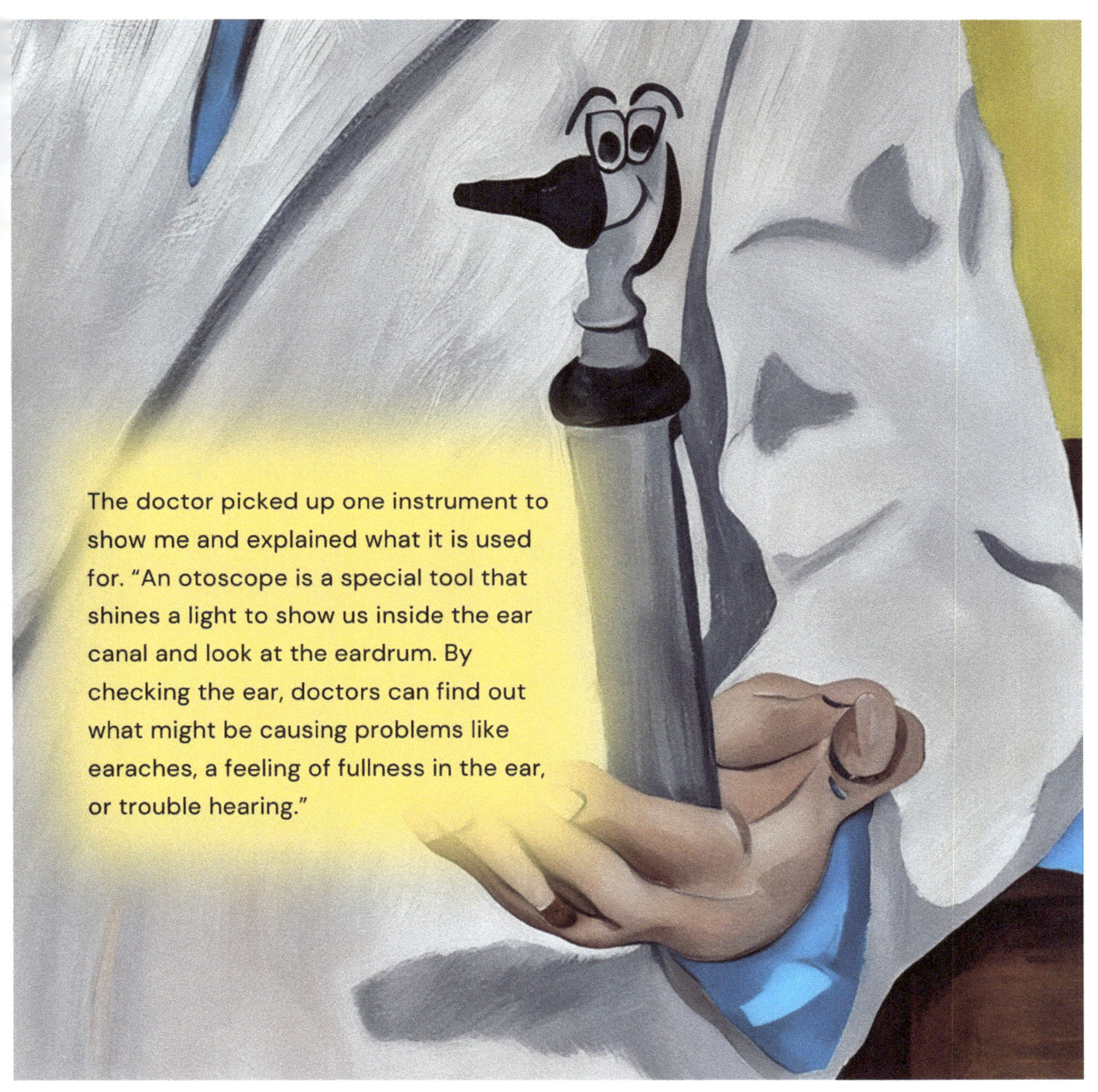

The doctor picked up one instrument to show me and explained what it is used for. "An otoscope is a special tool that shines a light to show us inside the ear canal and look at the eardrum. By checking the ear, doctors can find out what might be causing problems like earaches, a feeling of fullness in the ear, or trouble hearing."

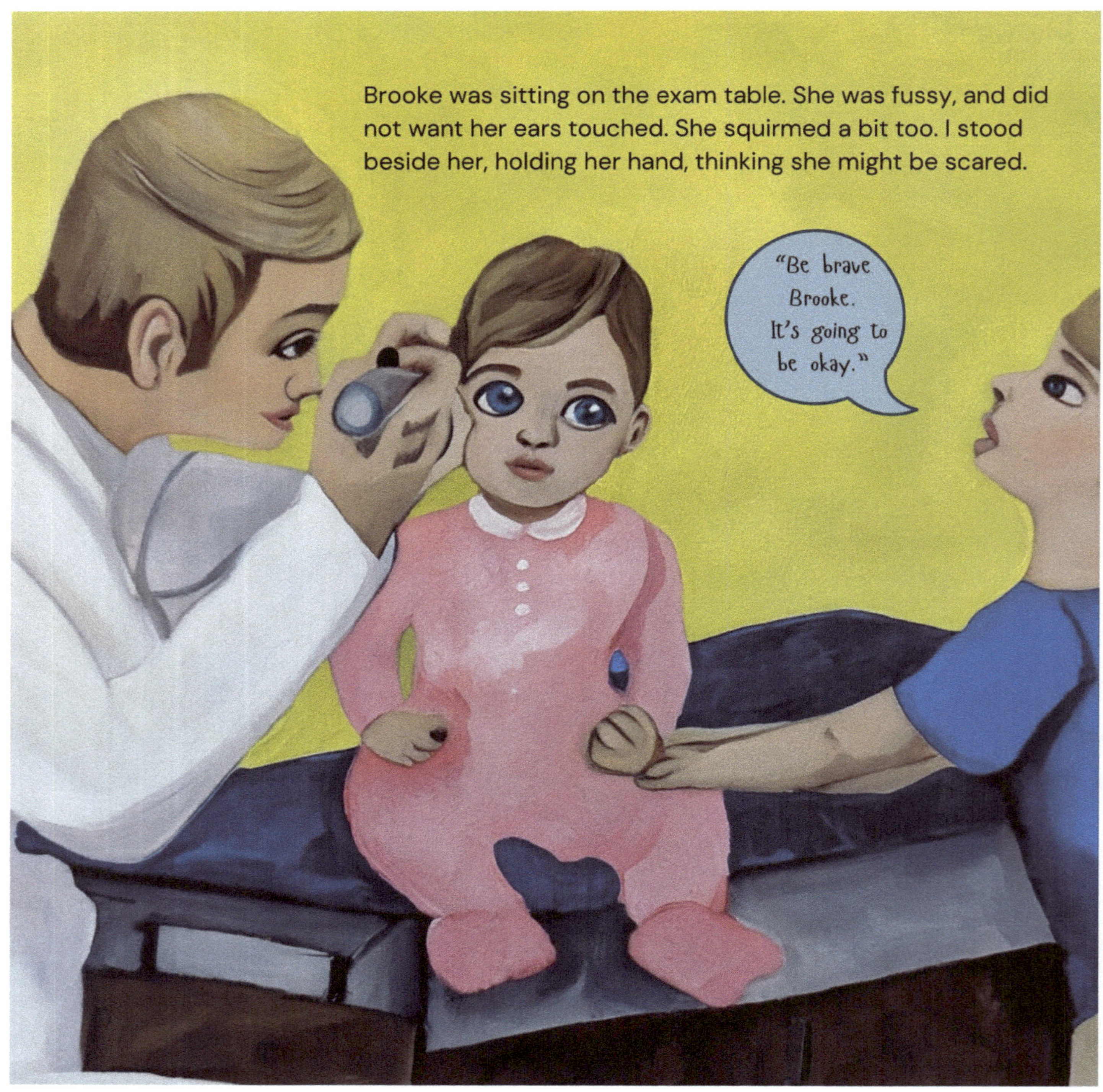

Brooke was sitting on the exam table. She was fussy, and did not want her ears touched. She squirmed a bit too. I stood beside her, holding her hand, thinking she might be scared.

The doctor reassured her, "This will tickle just a bit. It should not hurt." He then picked up the otoscope, switched the light on, and looked into her ear. I couldn't help but ask, "What do you see?"

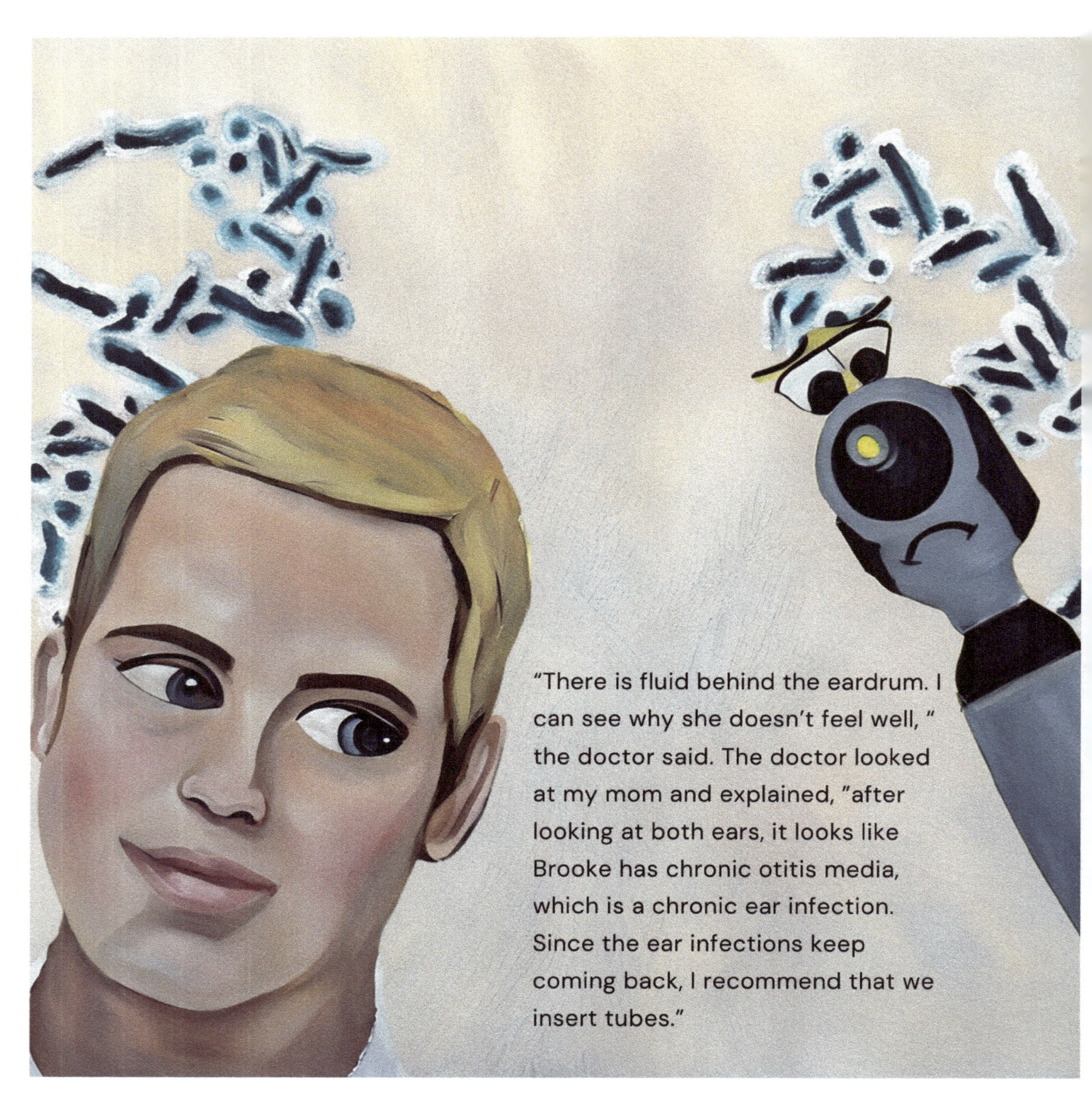

"There is fluid behind the eardrum. I can see why she doesn't feel well, " the doctor said. The doctor looked at my mom and explained, "after looking at both ears, it looks like Brooke has chronic otitis media, which is a chronic ear infection. Since the ear infections keep coming back, I recommend that we insert tubes."

What are ear
tubes?

Ear tubes resemble the same shape as a pool float or a donut.

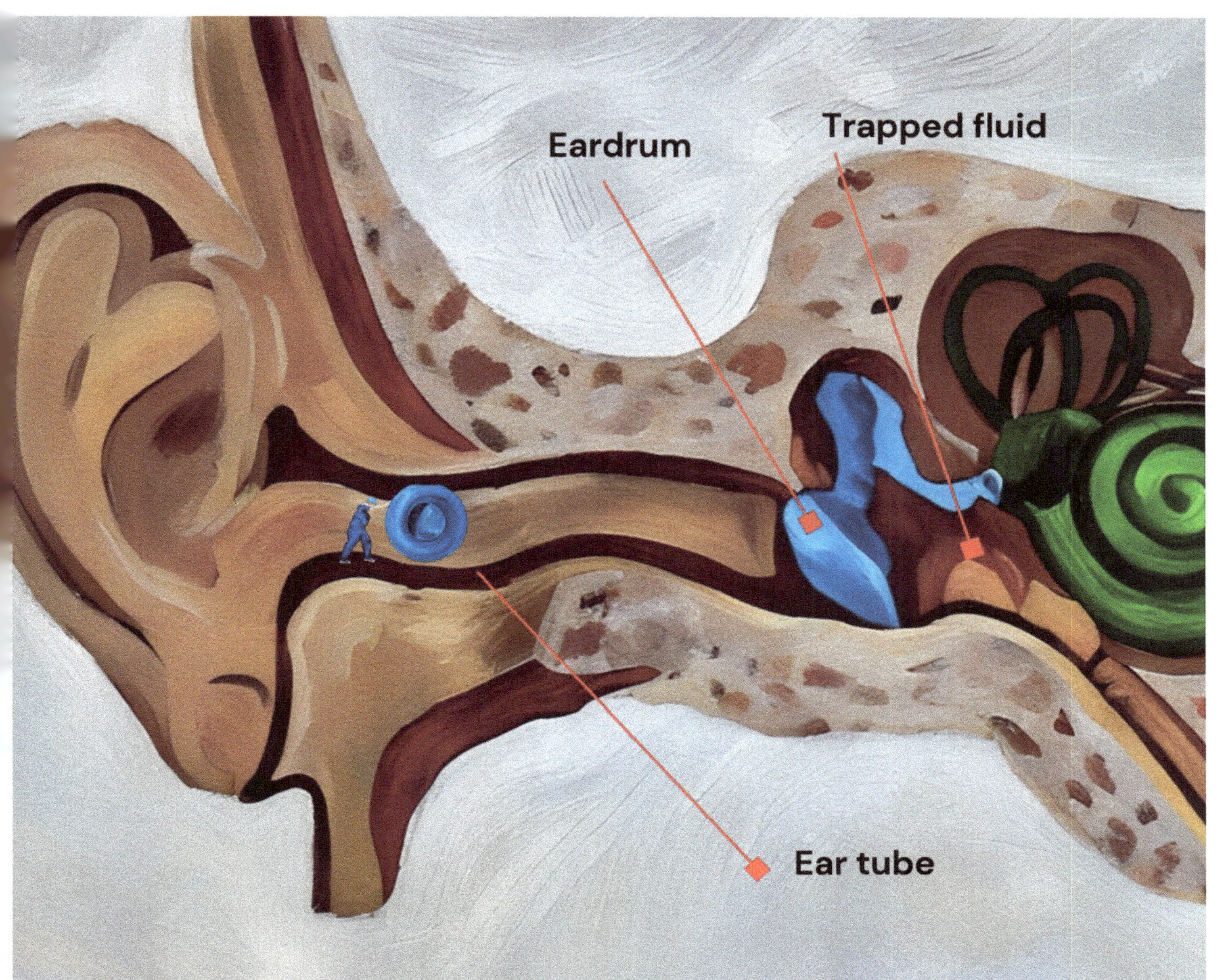

"Ear tubes sit in the eardrum and allow air to flow into the middle ear space allowing fluid to move freely without getting trapped" explained the doctor. I am a very curious kid. I had to ask him, "How will those tubes get in her ears?"

"Hey, I'm glad you asked! I have this book with pictures that can really help explain."
EAR-RESISTABLE WAYS TO FIX AN EAR INFECTION
TONSILS
all about ears
TYPES OF TUBES
jane gets her tonsils out

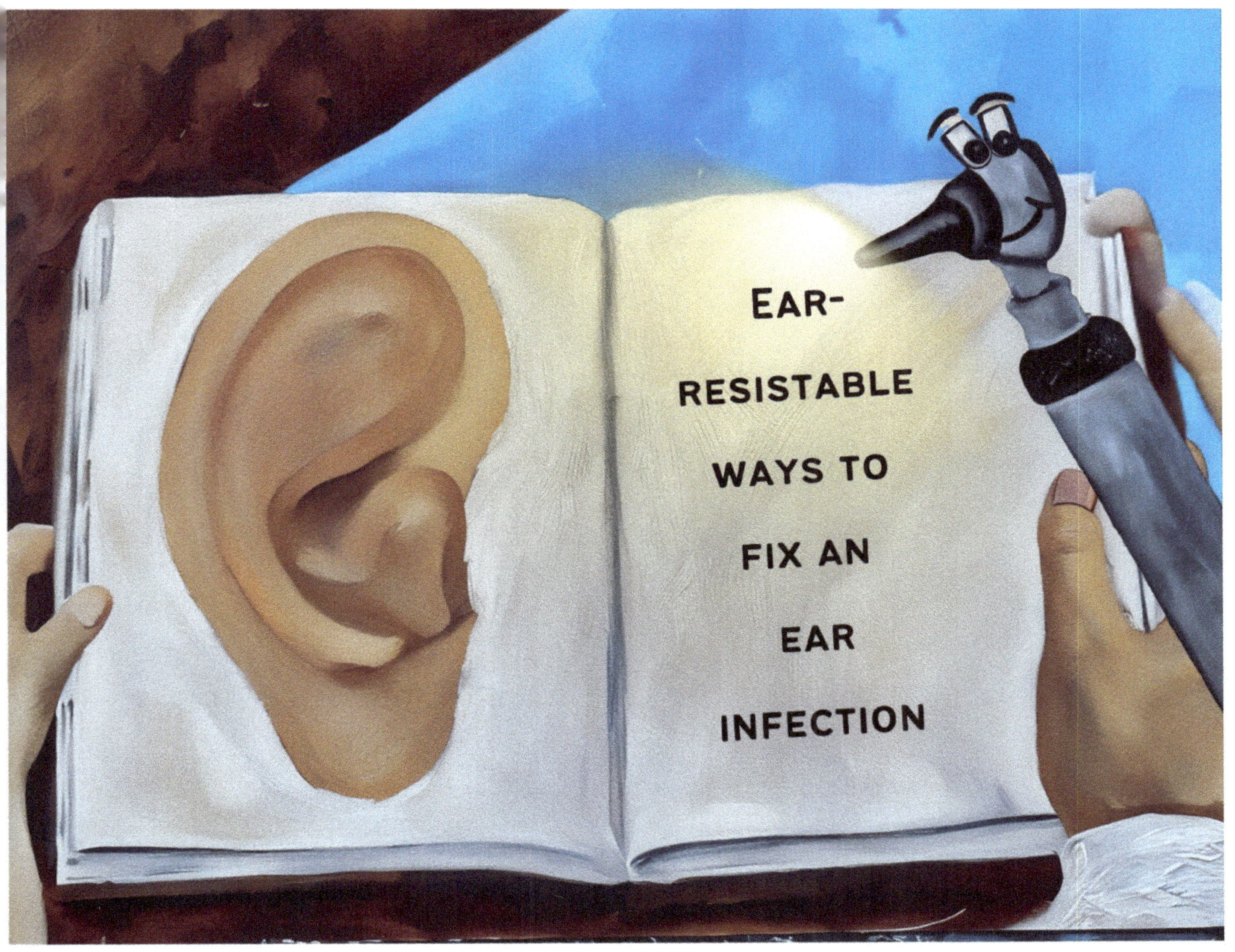

The doctor brought the book over to me and said "Let's take a look together, " as he opened the book.

"I will use a surgical microscope to help insert her ear tubes. A surgical microscope is like a super cool magnifying glass that doctors use when they perform really delicate surgeries. It helps us see tiny parts of the body, like the inside of your sister's ear, in a bright and clear way. This makes it easier for doctors to fix these little pieces, like the eardrum. "

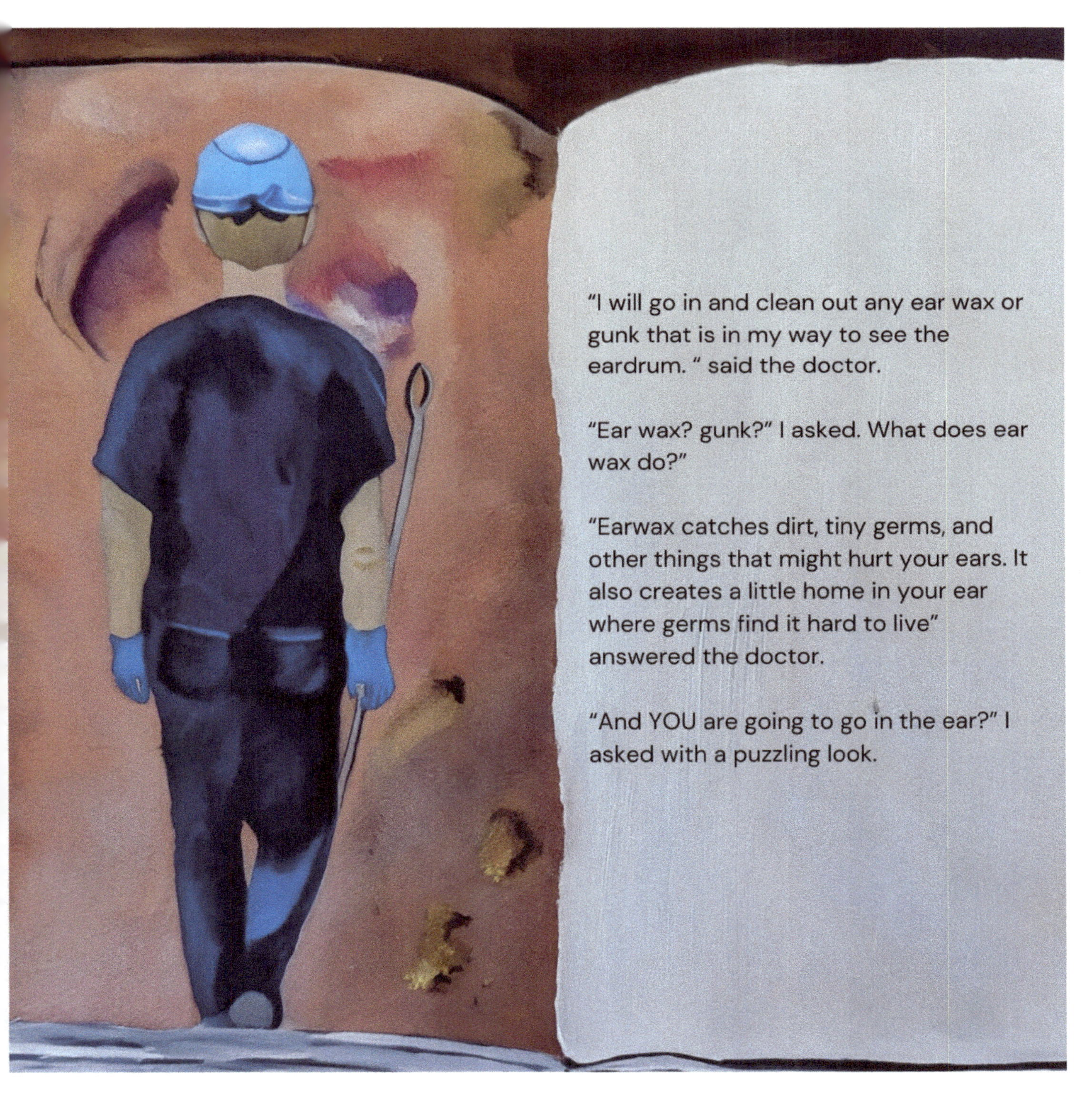

"I will go in and clean out any ear wax or gunk that is in my way to see the eardrum. " said the doctor.

"Ear wax? gunk?" I asked. What does ear wax do?"

"Earwax catches dirt, tiny germs, and other things that might hurt your ears. It also creates a little home in your ear where germs find it hard to live" answered the doctor.

"And YOU are going to go in the ear?" I asked with a puzzling look.

The doctor laughed. "I'm not going into the ear, but I will use instruments to do the job. When I see the eardrum, I will make a tiny opening, like a window in a wall, and put the tube in.

"Will my sister feel better after getting tubes?" I asked.
"Yes, with ear drops and the tubes, the fluid should not get stuck behind the eardrum. The fluid should move freely. " said the doctor.

"Ear drops too? I didn't know that it takes so much to make an ear feel better."

"There are just a few steps to improving the ear, the canal, and eardrum after surgery. Ear drops are liquid medicines for your ears. They can help with pain, swelling, infection, or too much earwax." stated the doctor.

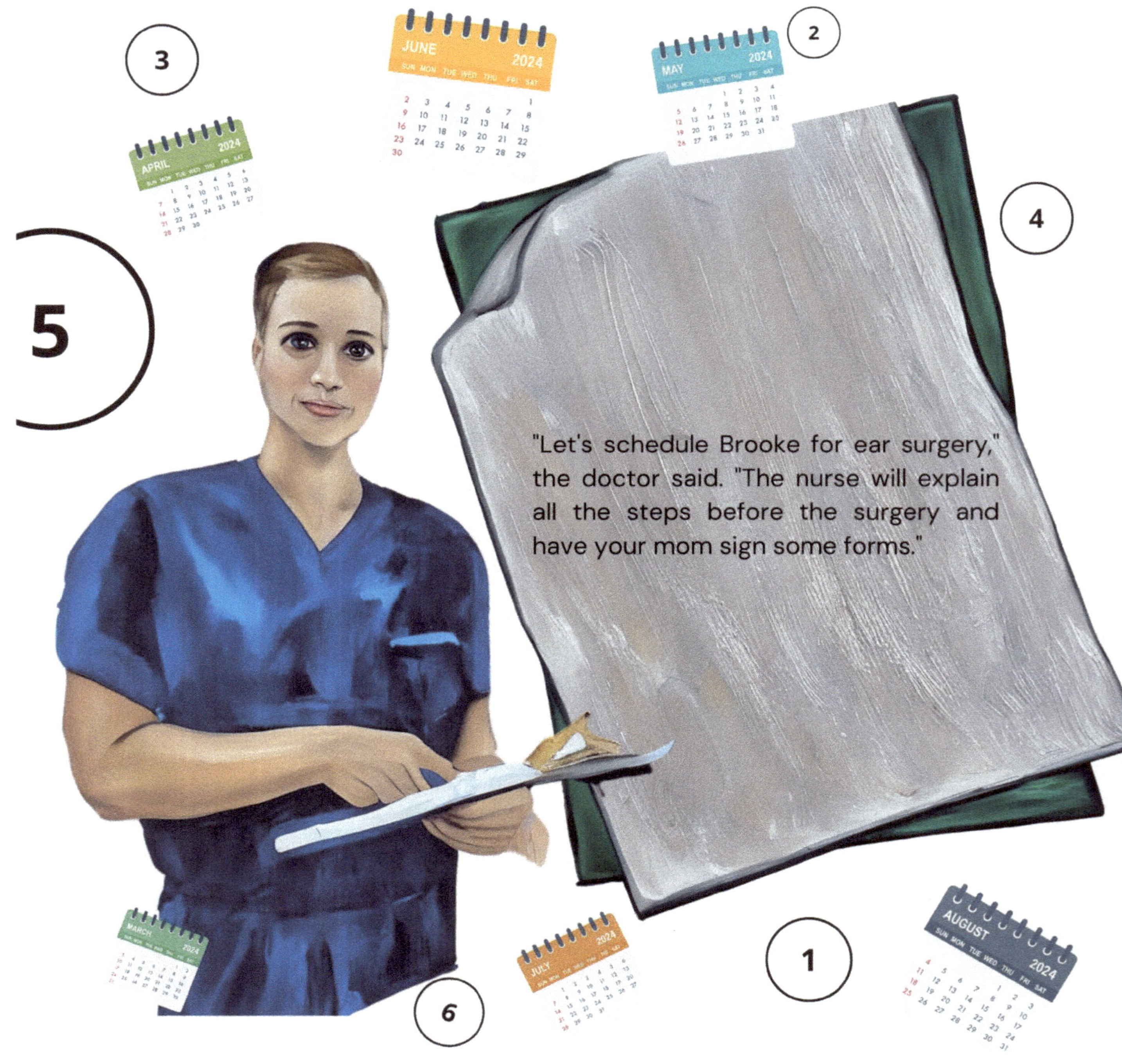
JUNE 2024
MAY 2024
APRIL 2024
MARCH 2024
JULY 2024
AUGUST 2024
"Let's schedule Brooke for ear surgery," the doctor said. "The nurse will explain all the steps before the surgery and have your mom sign some forms."

I asked my mom daily if it was time for Brooke's surgery, as I was anxious to see her recover and feel better.

Here we are at the surgery center! A nurse, dressed in blue and wearing a hat, brought us into a room with a warm smile. My mom had us both sit down on the bed. My sister was clinging to her blanket and seemed unsure about what was happening.

There was a TV on the wall showing cartoons, which caught my sister's attention for a little while. A nice nurse brought Brooke a gown and a hat to wear. She didn't really like the hat, though, so she ended up putting it on my head instead!

From the behind the curtain, a kind-hearted nurse appeared, her face beaming with a warm and welcoming smile. She gently offered Brooke a cozy blanket, ensuring she was comfortable and warm.

The doctor and another person called the anesthesia provider came to talk to my mom. They talked about what was going to happen during the surgery and how my mom would take care of my sister after the operation.

The curtain opened once more, revealing a different nurse who introduced herself as the Operating Room nurse. She asked my mom if she had any more questions. My mom replied that she didn't have any questions and seemed confident that my sister was in good hands. The operating room nurse pulled back the curtain and began to wheel the crib out of the room. Brooke looked back at Mom and me, waving goodbye.

In the operating room, the doctor reassured me that the anesthesia provider would gently put my sister to sleep. It's like taking a nap. Maybe she is counting sheep.

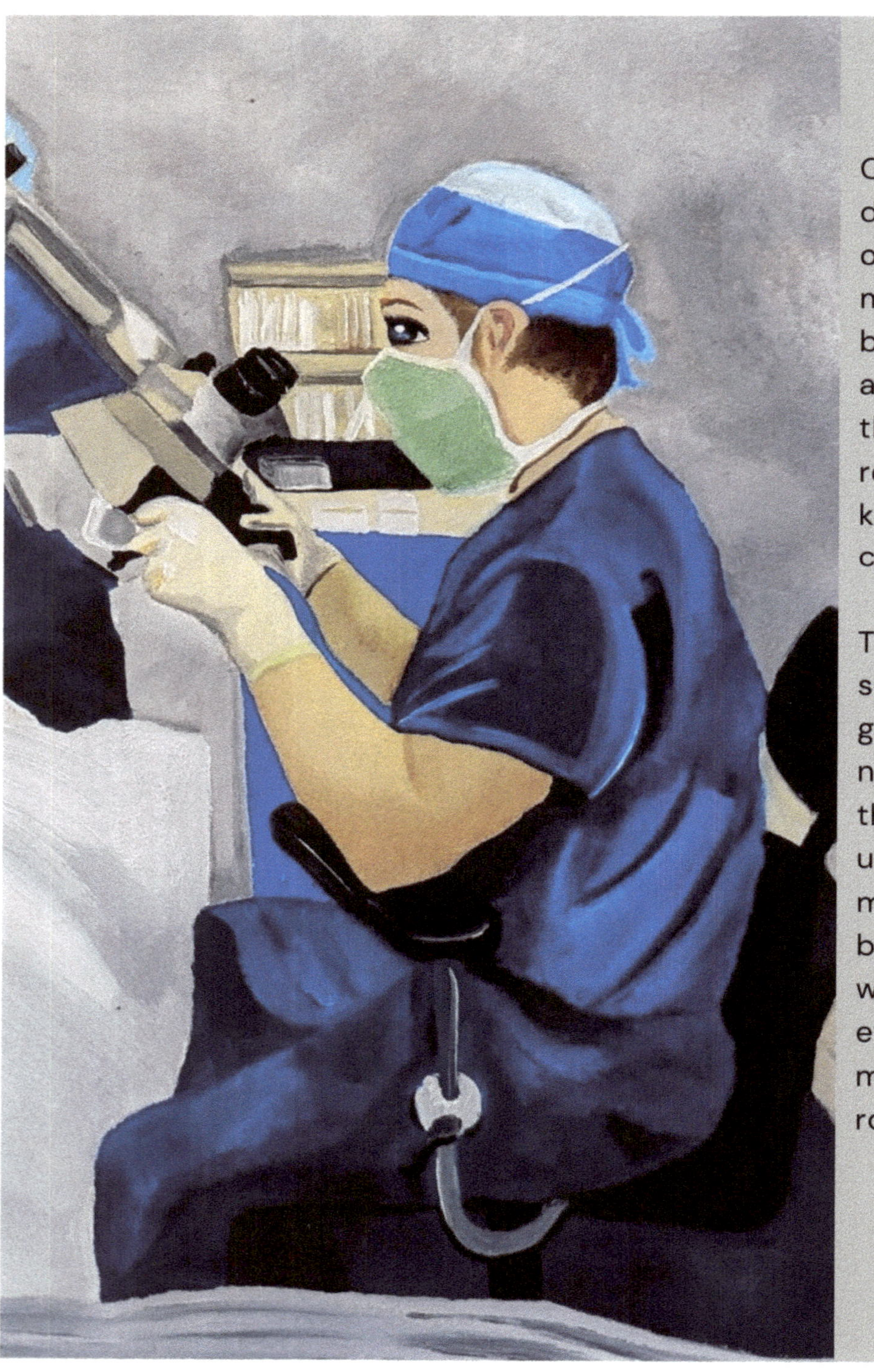

Once my sister was asleep, the doctor put a little tube in each of her ears and dropped some medicine in. They call this a bilateral myringotomy, which is a big medical word! It felt like the whole thing happened really fast. The next thing I knew, my sister was in a place called the Recovery Room.

The recovery room is a special spot in the hospital where kids go right after their surgery. The nurses and doctors watch over them to make sure they wake up okay from the sleepy medicine and start to feel better. It's like a safe place where they can check if everything is alright before moving them to their regular room.

The nurses gentle words cut through the hum and beeps of the machines as they lovingly held and comforted her.

I peeked through the door and observed the nurses caring for my sister, who was still peacefully asleep. She was connected to a monitor that beeped every few seconds, while one of the nurses gently held her hand.

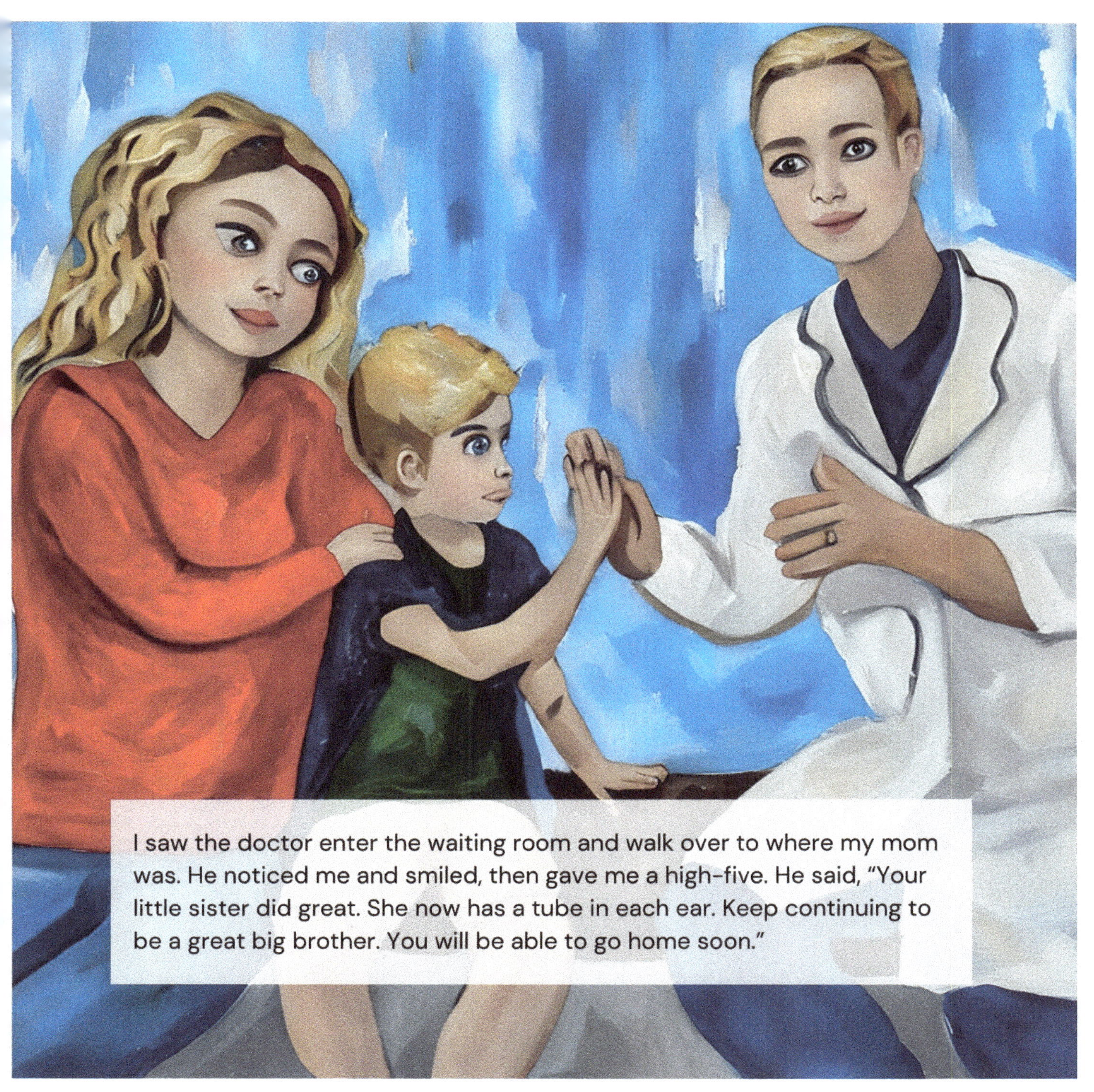

I saw the doctor enter the waiting room and walk over to where my mom was. He noticed me and smiled, then gave me a high-five. He said, "Your little sister did great. She now has a tube in each ear. Keep continuing to be a great big brother. You will be able to go home soon."

Recovery

A nurse walked into the room carrying papers and a cup of juice. She reviewed some important information and handed my mother a piece of paper containing my sister's ear drop prescription.

From the hallway, I could hear faint cries; my sister was on her way. She was upset and wailing. The nurse gently placed Brooke in my mother's arms. My mom held her close and comforted her until the tears subsided. To soothe her, Mom offered her some juice from the cup.

It's been a few days, and my sister has returned to her usual self. She is running and playing joyfully, laughing and following me around once more. There's no tugging at her ears, no signs of fever, and she isn't crying with tears. She's clearly on the road to recovery.

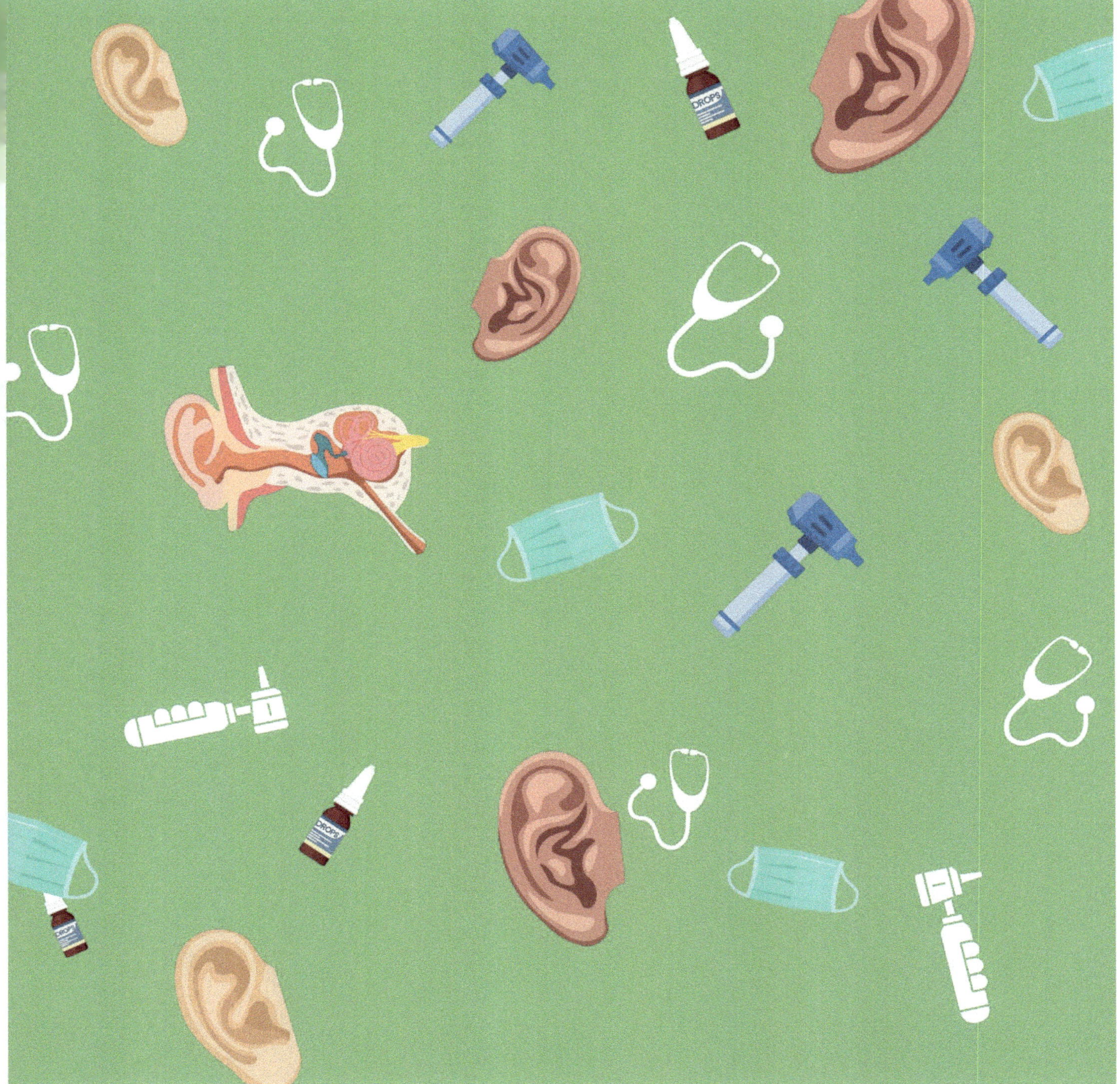

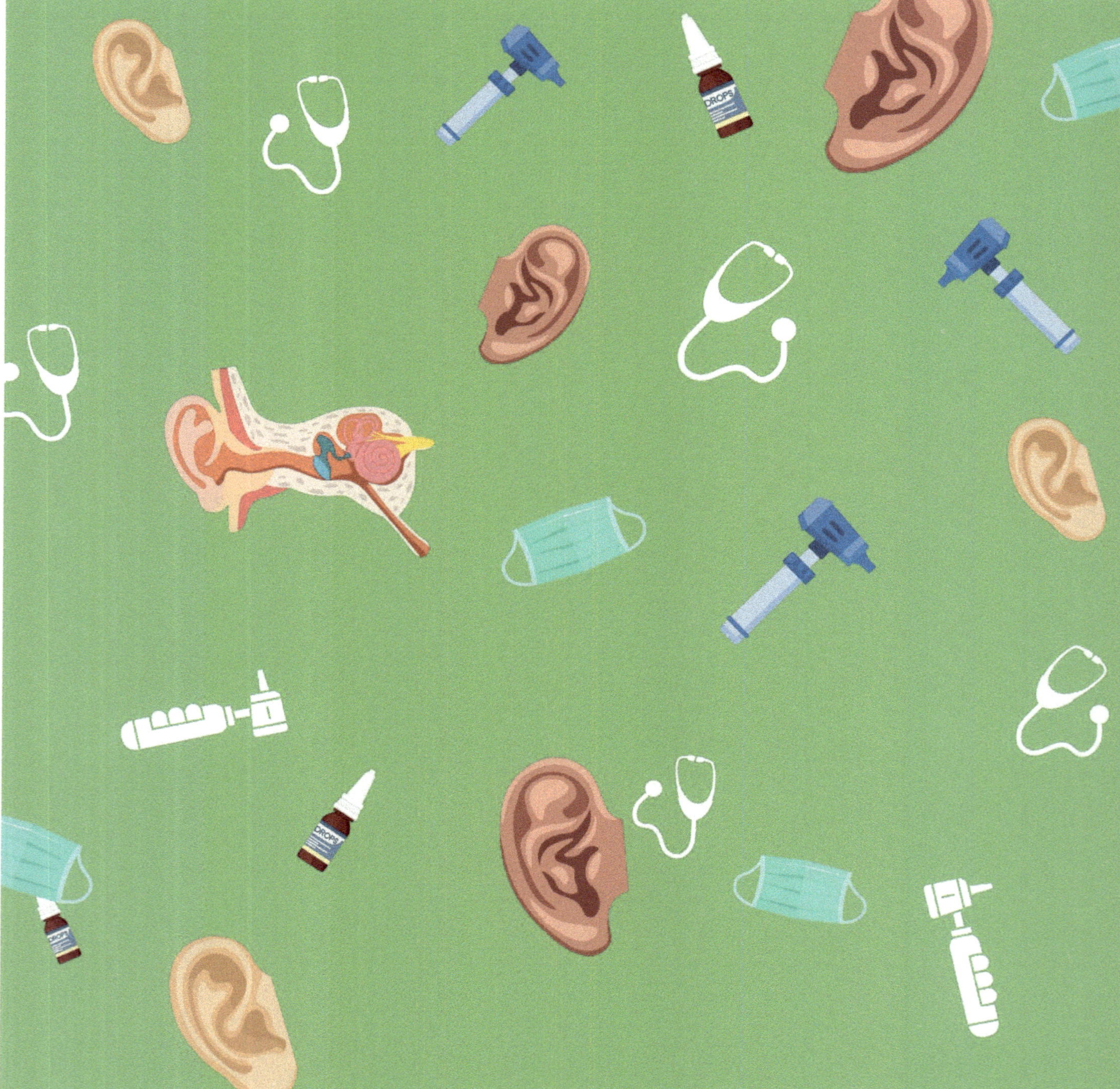